The Most Up-to-date Pocket Guide to Discover the Hidden Treasures of Assisi, Culture, Must-See Attraction Sites and Insider Tips for First-Timers

Bonus: Christmas Holiday Celebration And 30 Exciting Things To Do In Assisi

Assisi

Travel Guide 2023-2024

ROLAND RICHARD

Table of Contents

Saint francis of Assisi Statue

Introduction

Welcome to Assisi, a location rich in spirituality, history, and scenic beauty that will make your trip here really unforgettable. You will be getting all the knowledge you need in this guide to help you get the most out of your trip to this adorable Italian town.

Greetings From Assisi

As soon as you set foot in Assisi, you'll feel as though time has stopped for you. With its congested, twisting alleyways, stone structures covered in historic paintings, and the calming sound of church bells resonating through the air, this mediaeval town is a walking museum. There is an obvious sense of history here, and the ultimate destination promises not only a journey through space but also one through time.

Why Visit Assisi?

Apart from its magical Christmas, why would you decide to travel to Assisi? Here are a few convincing justifications:

★ **Spiritual Centre:** Saint Francis, one of the most renowned individuals in the Christian world, was born in Assisi. The cultural fabric of the town is intricately linked with the town's religious significance.

The beautiful Basilica of Saint Francis, which contains the saint's relics, and the Basilica of Saint Clare, which is named after another revered local saint, are both open to visitors.

★ **Cultural Heritage:** UNESCO has designated Assisi's old town as a World Heritage Site. The town's ancient Rocca Maggiore castle, famous artist murals like those by Giotto, and mediaeval architecture all attest to its lengthy past. The yearly Calendimaggio event in Assisi, which features parades and mediaeval reenactments, is evidence of the city's vibrant culture.

★ *Scenic Beauty:* Assisi is surrounded by rolling hills, olive orchards, and vineyards, making it the ideal vacation spot for those who love the outdoors. From numerous vantage points across the town, the views of the Umbrian countryside are just breathtaking. Its attraction is enhanced by the peaceful surroundings and the availability of outdoor pursuits like cycling and hiking.

★ *Culinary Delights:* Italian cuisine is well-known around the world, and Assisi is no exception. The town's eateries and trattorias provide an opportunity to sample traditional Umbrian meals, regional wines, and handcrafted goods. Don't pass up the chance to experience real Italian flavours while you're there.

How to Use This Guide

This guide has been designed to help you get the most out of your visit to Assisi:

★ ***Chapters and Sections:*** This guide is divided into sections, each of which focuses on a distinct aspect of Assisi. To quickly and easily find a certain piece of information, use the table of contents.

★ ***Itinerary Options:*** Based on the length of your visit, we offer suggested itineraries in Chapter 5. These itineraries will enable you to make the most of your time in Assisi, whether you have one, two, or three days available.

★ *Insider Advice:* You'll find insider advice to improve your experience throughout Chapter 7. You will find hidden gems and make the most of your time in Assisi by following this advice from residents and seasoned tourists.

Travel Requirements

Keep in mind the following practical information before starting your trip to Assisi:

1. **Passport and Visa:** Make sure your passport is valid for at least six months after the date you intend to depart. The same goes for your visa. Before leaving for Italy, find out if you need a visa and apply for one in advance if you do.

2. **Currency:** Italy recognises the Euro (EUR) as its official currency. Despite the widespread acceptance of credit cards, it is still a good idea to carry some

cash, especially for smaller purchases and in more isolated locations.

3. **Language:** The predominant language used in Assisi is Italian. Even though many locals working in the tourism sector have knowledge of English, knowing a few simple Italian words is usually appreciated. It can improve your interactions and make it easier for you to go around town.

4. **Climate:** Assisi experiences a Mediterranean climate. To make sure you have the right attire for the season, check the weather prediction for the dates of your trip before you pack. When touring the town's cobblestone streets, don't forget to bring some comfortable walking shoes.

5. **Safety:** Travellers can feel secure visiting Assisi in general. However, it's a good idea to exercise common sense caution, like protecting your

possessions and paying attention to your surroundings. The residents are polite and helpful, and the town is renowned for its inviting attitude.

Now that you have read this introduction, you are ready to start your Assisi experience. As you discover the cultural treasures, must-see sights, and hidden gems of this unique town, this guide is your reliable travel companion.

Have fun on your trip, and may Assisi leave you with enduring memories of awe!

Chapter 1

Preparing for Your Trip

To ensure a seamless and pleasurable trip, careful planning is required before you leave for Assisi. We'll go over everything you need to know to get ready for your Assisi trip in this part.

Making Your Travel Plans

Making the most of your trip requires careful planning because Assisi has a wide range of attractions and activities. How to do it is as follows:

1. *Research:* Start by learning about the top sights and things to do in Assisi as revealed in this guide. Take into account your preferences and areas of interest, whether they involve visiting historical places, going

on outdoor excursions, or dining on regional cuisine.

2. *Duration:* Determine the number of days you'll stay in Assisi. Even though you can see the main attractions in a single day, staying longer provides for more in-depth investigation and a more leisurely experience.

3. *Customize:* Create a personalised itinerary based on your preferences. Give museums and historic sites more of your time if you enjoy history. Outdoor activities like hiking or wine tasting in the countryside might be appropriate for nature lovers.

4. *Balance:* Maintain a healthy ratio of leisure time to planned activities. Allow time for random meetings and relaxing walks through the town's picturesque streets.

5. *Apply Itinerary Advice:* In Chapter 6, we offer proposed itineraries for one, two, and three days in Assisi. These can act as the basis for your plans.

The Ideal Season to Visit Assisi

Your experience in Assisi can be substantially impacted by the time of your visit. Here is a list of the ideal dates to visit this lovely town:

★ *Spring (March to May):* Assisi is frequently visited during the spring. The environment comes to life with blooming flowers and lush vegetation as a result of the excellent weather. The weather is perfect for enjoying outdoor activities and the town's splendour.

★ *Summer (June to August):* Summer is a popular travel time. Even when it's warm and sunny outside, the town might get busy. At popular attractions, be ready for higher costs and longer wait times.

★ *Autumn (September to November):* This season is also a top choice for travel. The surrounding vineyards of Assisi are currently in full harvest, and the weather is still good. For fans of wine, the time is right.

★ *Winter (December to February):* Assisi experiences pleasant, albeit occasionally frigid, winters. This time of year is less busy in the town, making it a tranquil period for touring historic places. ***Assisi has a particularly magical Christmas.***

Entry Requirements and Visas

Make sure you have the required visas and entrance paperwork before travelling to Assisi. Here are some important things to think about:

1. **Visa Requirements:** Check the criteria for an Italian visa based on your nationality. Make sure your passport is valid for at least six months after the day you plan to depart.

2. **Schengen Area:** Italy is a member of the Schengen Area, which permits travellers to roam freely among its member nations. Make sure you have the necessary visa or entrance clearance if you intend to travel to other Schengen nations.

3. **Travel Insurance:** Consider obtaining travel insurance that includes coverage for medical emergencies, trip cancellations, and lost baggage. It's a sensible precaution for cross-border travel.

Vaccines and Wellness Advice

It is crucial to protect your health and well-being while travelling. Here are a few health-related points to think about: Examine any recommended or needed immunisations or health measures for visitors to Italy.

1. **Prescription Drugs:** If you need to take prescription drugs, make sure you have cnough for the duration of your trip. Carry them with labels that are clear in their original containers.

2. **Healthcare:** Medical services are available in Assisi, but it's a good idea to carry travel insurance that includes coverage for unexpected medical costs. Just in case, become familiar with where the nearest pharmacies and medical facilities are located.

3. **Hydration and Sun Protection:** Stay hydrated, especially during the summer, and shield your skin from the sun by wearing sunscreen and appropriate clothing.

Packing Tips

Being well-prepared for your vacation might increase your convenience and comfort. Consider bringing the following goods to Assisi:

1. *Clothing:* Dress appropriately for the weather based on the time of year you will be visiting. Because Assisi's streets are frequently cobblestone, you must wear comfortable walking shoes.

2. *Adapters and Converters:* Italy uses Type C and Type F electrical outlets. Adapters and converters are required. If your equipment requires a different type of plug or a different voltage, bring the appropriate adapters and converters.

3. *Travel Documents:* Travel documents, such as your passport, visa, trip insurance, and itinerary, should

be organised. You can create a digital backup if necessary

4. *Local Currency:* Although credit cards are extensively used, keeping some local currency on hand is useful for small purchases or locations that don't accept cards.

5. *Reusable Water Bottle:* Carry a reusable water bottle to stay hydrated while cutting down on plastic trash.

6. *Medications and First Aid:* Bring any necessary medications, a small first-aid kit, and any over-the-counter medications you may require.

You are now prepared to organise your vacation to Assisi. Assisi has something to offer every traveller, regardless of whether they are drawn to it for its spiritual legacy, cultural diversity, or natural beauty.

Have fun on your trip, and may Assisi bring you many amazing experiences and discoveries.

Assisi, Church, Italy

Chapter 2

Cultural Overview of Assisi

Your travel experience will be enhanced if you are aware of Assisi's cultural setting. We explore the town's fascinating history, distinctive culture, and monetary system in this section, as well as offer important travel and safety advice.

The Long History of Assisi

The interesting events and influences that have fashioned Assisi's history into the tapestry it is today are explained in the summary below:

★ *Ancient Origins:* Assisi's history dates back to when it was an Umbrian town called Asisium. In the first century BC, it later evolved into a Roman colony.

★ *The Glory of the Mediaeval Ages:* Assisi flourished during the Middle Ages as a hub of art, culture, and spirituality. Saint Francis and Saint Clare, two illustrious members of the Catholic Church, were born and lived during this period.

★ *Renaissance and Beyond:* Assisi experienced additional advancements in both art and architecture during the Renaissance. The town's churches and other structures prominently display its rich legacy.

★ *UNESCO World Heritage Site:* In 2000, Assisi's historic centre received this honour in recognition of its exceptional cultural significance and the preservation of its mediaeval character.

Local Customs and Culture

The historical and religious significance of Assisi has a significant impact on its culture. Here are some notable cultural examples:

★ *Religious Heritage:* Because of its connections to Saint Francis and Saint Clare, Assisi is a popular pilgrimage destination for Catholics all over the world. A notable religious occasion is the Feast of Saint Francis, which is observed in the first part of October.

★ *Calendimaggio Festival:* The annual Calendimaggio festival in Assisi, usually held in May, contains mediaeval reenactments, parades, and competitions that give guests a look into the town's rich history.

★ *Cuisine:* Food plays a significant role in Assisi culture. Try local specialities including truffles, olive oil, and Sagrantino wines. Traditional foods like "strangozzi al Tartufo" (pasta with truffle sauce) shouldn't be missed.

★ *Art and Craftsmanship:* Assisi has a long history of artistic and skilled workmanship. Local craftsmen can be found creating handmade ceramics, textiles, and other goods that are frequently influenced by mediaeval patterns.

Currency and Language

● *Language:* Italian is the city of Assisi's official language. Even though English is frequently used in the tourism sector, it is always welcomed when visitors attempt to speak a few simple Italian words. Here are some key terms and expressions:

- *Buongiorno (Good morning)*

- *Buonasera (Good evening)*

- *Grazie (Thank you)*

- *Per favore (Please)*

- *Parla inglese? (Do you speak English?)*

★ *Currency:* The Euro (EUR) is the official unit of exchange in Assisi and throughout Italy. It's wise to have some cash on hand for smaller transactions and for situations where a credit card might not be accepted. ATMs are commonly available for cash withdrawals and currency conversions.

Travel and Safety Advice

Although Assisi is generally a safe place to visit, it's nevertheless wise to follow this safety advice:

1. *Pickpocketing:* Pickpocketing is not a widespread occurrence in Assisi, but it is always advisable to

exercise caution in crowded areas and popular tourist destinations. Watch out for your possessions, especially in crowded situations.

2. *Emergency Numbers:* Police in Italy can be reached in an emergency at 112. Call 118 in case of medical emergencies. For easy access, save these phone numbers.

3. *Local Customs:* Respect for regional traditions and customs. Dress modestly, covering your knees and shoulders, when visiting churches and other sacred buildings.

4. *Health Caution:* Make sure your travel insurance includes coverage for unexpected medical expenses. Learn where the nearest pharmacies and medical facilities are located.

5. *Transportation Security:* If you plan to drive in the historic district, be aware that parking spaces are

scarce and the streets are winding. To prevent tickets from being towed, park only in designated zones.

With the help of this cultural overview, you have learned a lot about the background, customs, and everyday life in Assisi. You'll have a greater understanding of the town's cultural significance and be more ready for a secure and pleasurable visit as you explore it.

Enjoy your exploration of Assisi's culture!

Chapter 3

Discovering Assisi

Assisi is a hidden gem of history, culture, and beauty whose secrets are just begging to be discovered. We'll walk you through the must-see sights and undiscovered jewels that make Assisi a special place in this part of the guide.

Must-See Attractions

There are lots of must-see sites in Assisi that highlight the town's significant historical and cultural heritage. Here are a few of the best:

Saint Francis Basilica

GPS Location: Latitude 43.0708, Longitude 12.6176

Estimated Cost: Entry to the Upper Basilica - €5-€10, Entry to the Lower Basilica - €3-€6

The jewel of Assisi's crown is the Basilica of Saint Francis (Basilica di San Francesco). It is a UNESCO World Heritage Site and honours Saint Francis, the patron saint of Italy. Relevant information includes:

The Upper Basilica: Beautiful frescoes by well-known artists like Giotto and Cimabue adorn this higher church. A masterwork of mediaeval art, the frescoes depict scenes from Saint Francis' life.

The Lower Basilica: The tomb of Saint Francis is located in the lower church. The basilica's architecture and frescoes contribute to its spiritual and artistic depth.

Courtyard and Views: Take advantage of the lovely courtyard between the top and lower basilicas, which provides sweeping views of Assisi and the surrounding area.

Rocca Maggiore

GPS Location: Latitude 43.0717, Longitude 12.6193

Estimated Cost: Entry - €5-€8

A mediaeval fortification called Rocca Maggiore rises over Assisi and provides stunning views of both the city and the Umbrian countryside. Exploring the fortress allows you to:

Immerse Yourself In History: Rocca Maggiore's well-preserved walls, towers, and buildings can be used to learn about its past. The fortress has been important to Assisi's history.

Scenic Overlook: Reach the highest point for breathtaking 360-degree vistas. It's a great place to take pictures and enjoy the beautiful scenery.

Museum: Discover the fortress's modest museum, which houses artefacts and offers historical context for Assisi.

San Rufino Cathedral (Assisi Cathedral)

GPS Location: Latitude 43.0707, Longitude 12.6163

Estimated Cost: Entry - €3-€5

The San Rufino Cathedral, usually referred to as the Assisi Cathedral, is a masterpiece of Romanesque architecture and a significant place of worship in Assisi.

Architectural Beauty: Stunning Romanesque architecture, including elaborate facades and a rose window, can be found in the cathedral.

Religious Significance: Saint Clare and Saint Rufinus of Assisi are honoured at the cathedral. You'll discover a serene and important spiritual area inside.

Baptistery: Visit the Baptistery, which is nearby and famous for its baptismal font and lovely frescoes.

Discovering Assisi's Hidden Gems

While Assisi's must-see sites are unquestionably amazing, the town also contains undiscovered gems that offer a deeper insight into its personality and culture. The next information will provide you with all you need to enjoy your travel and deepen the Assisi experience you are craving.

Beautiful Neighbourhoods

Beyond its well-known sites, Assisi also has attractive neighbourhoods. Wander through the following:

- *Rione San Paolo (GPS Location: Latitude 43.0717, Longitude 12.6176):* This area provides a window into daily life in the area. Explore its quaint shops, meander through its winding streets, and chat with the locals.

- *Rione San Francesco (GPS Location: Latitude 43.0702, Longitude 12.6143):* Take a stroll around the Saint Francis Basilica. The serene area has lovely views and undiscovered nooks just waiting to be found.

- *Rione Borgo Aretino (GPS Location: Latitude 43.0706, Longitude 12.6173):* This area is renowned for its old homes and artisan studios.

Skilful artisans produce textiles, ceramics, and other regional goods.

Workshops for Artisans

Estimated Price: Depends on Purchases

A strong artist community creates top-notch handicrafts in Assisi. Consider going to the following:

- *Ceramic Workshops (GPS Location: Latitude 43.0696, Longitude 12.6167):* Assisi is renowned for its vibrant ceramics. Visit the studios where artists produce ceramics, tiles, and furnishings. You may even buy original mementoes.

- *Textile and Weaving Studios (GPS Location: Latitude 43.0710, Longitude 12.6146):* Discover the craft of ancient Umbrian weaving at the textile and weaving studios. There are several handwoven textiles for sale, such as scarves, tablecloths, and more.

Gastronomic Delights

Estimated Cost: Dependent on dining options

A fun experience is discovering Assisi's food scene. Make sure to enjoy local cuisine and flavours:

- *Trattorias and Osterias (GPS Location: Latitude 43.0708, Longitude 12.6171)*: Dine at nearby trattorias and osterias to sample authentic Umbrian food. Try meals like "torta al testo" (a kind of flatbread) and "pappardelle al cinghiale" (wild boar pasta).

- *Wine Tasting (GPS Location: Latitude 43.0672, Longitude 12.6078)*: The area around Assisi is home to many vineyards that produce top-notch wines, including the renowned Sagrantino. To taste these local delights, go on a wine tour.

- *Food Markets (GPS Location: Latitude 43.0710, Longitude 12.6172)*: Visit the neighbourhood food markets to sample artisanal cheeses, fresh fruits and vegetables, and extra virgin olive oil. The Piazza del Comune frequently hosts markets and food fairs. You may be lucky to come across one of these events being held.

Chapter 4

Experiencing Assisi

A fascinating fusion of Assisi's history, culture, and culinary delights is presented. Everyone is invited to immerse themselves in the spirit of Assisi in this section, which offers a tapestry of encounters that will forever change the course of your trip.

Outdoor Activities

The scenic surroundings and natural beauty of Assisi provide a wide range of outdoor pursuits to revitalise your spirit.

A. Hiking in the Apennines: Explore Umbria's Heart

GPS Location: Latitude 43.0705, Longitude 12.6395

A playground of picturesque routes awaits keen hikers in Assisi, which serves as a gateway to the magnificent Apennine Mountains. Embark on the renowned "Sentiero Francescano" (French Path) by entering the Monte Subasio Regional Park.

This ancient path leads you through hermitages, through verdant woodlands, and provides expansive views of the Umbrian countryside. It's a voyage that follows in Saint Francis's footsteps.

B. Cycling Tours: Ride by vineyards and olive groves

GPS Location: Latitude 43.0645, Longitude 12.6118

Exploring the area by bicycle is an amazing way to take in Assisi's beautiful scenery. The "Strada del Vino" (Wine Road) travels over undulating hills filled with olive trees and vineyards. Rent a bike and follow it. Visit lovely wineries along the way for wine tastings to experience the rich flavours of the region's Sagrantino wine, which is famous for its powerful personality.

C. Wine Tasting: Sample the Liquid Gold of Umbria

- *GPS Location (Cantina Dionigi): Latitude 43.0656, Longitude 12.6147*
- *GPS Location (Terre Margaritelli): Latitude 43.0343, Longitude 12.5772*

Wine tasting is an art form in Assisi, where some of Italy's finest wines are produced. For a tour through Umbria's viticultural past, visit the charming Cantina Dionigi or the renowned Terre Margaritelli wineries. As you taste velvety reds and crisp whites against a backdrop of rolling hills covered in vines, let your palate serve as your guide.

Arts and Culture

Immerse yourself in the diverse artistic manifestations that make up Assisi's rich cultural tapestry:

A. Music and Festivals: Harmonies Among Mediaeval Splendour

- *Calendimaggio Festival GPS Location (Historic Center): Latitude 43.0717, Longitude 12.6187*
- *Assisi Festival GPS Location (Various Venues): Latitude 43.0701, Longitude 12.6154*

The mediaeval appeal of Assisi serves as the ideal setting for a schedule packed with exciting festivals and musical events. The town is transformed into a mediaeval wonderland during the Calendimaggio festival in May, complete with jousting contests, processions, and lovely music. The Assisi Festival, which takes place in July, provides classical music performances in beautiful old buildings, giving your cultural experience a timeless touch.

B. Museums and Galleries: A Window into the Soul of Assisi

- *Museo della Porziuncola GPS Location: Latitude 43.0657, Longitude 12.6197*
- *Pinacoteca Comunale GPS Location: Latitude 43.0710, Longitude 12.6159*

Visit the museums and galleries in Assisi to immerse yourself in the city's historical and cultural treasures. Ancient manuscripts and artefacts from the Franciscan past are displayed in the Museo della Porziuncola. You'll be mesmerised by stunning works of art that span decades at the Pinacoteca Comunale, featuring masterpieces by well-known Italian painters.

C. Local Arts and Crafts: Wonders of the Artisan

- *Ceramic Workshop GPS Location (Rione Borgo Aretino): Latitude 43.0698, Longitude 12.6154*
- *Textile and Weaving Studio GPS Location (Rione San Francesco): Latitude 43.0709, Longitude 12.6145*

The vibrant artisan community in Assisi reflects the city's artistic spirit. Discover the vibrantly coloured, intricately designed artisan pottery at Rione Borgo Aretino. Find weaving and textile studios in Rione San Francesco where master weavers create wonderful fabrics, such as scarves and tablecloths.

Gastronomic Journeys

The food scene of Assisi is a journey of flavours ready to be experienced:

A. Savouring Umbria's Culinary Delights in Assisi

Piazza del Comune GPS Location: Latitude 43.0709, Longitude 12.6151

The cuisine of Assisi is a representation of Umbrian culinary customs. To enjoy foods like "torta al testo," a rustic flatbread, and "strangozzi al Tartufo," a delicious pasta with truffle sauce, dive into neighbourhood trattorias and osterias. Visit the busy Piazza del Comune, where food markets provide handmade treats, fresh produce, cheeses, and olive oil.

B. Authentic Recipes: Mastering the Techniques of Umbrian Cooking

Casa Zunino GPS Location: Latitude 43.0714, Longitude 12.6165

Experience a gastronomic journey by enrolling in hands-on cooking lessons where professional chefs reveal the secrets of age-old Umbrian dishes. You're invited to make traditional meals like "pappardelle al cinghiale," pasta with wild boar sauce, and "bruschetta al Tartufo," toast with truffle oil, at Casa Zunino, a beautiful culinary institute.

C. Dining Advice - Enjoy Every Bite

- *Il Frantoio GPS Location: Latitude 43.0707, Longitude 12.6150*
- *Ristorante Metastasio GPS Location: Latitude 43.0715, Longitude 12.6164*

A unique sensory experience awaits you when you eat in Assisi. There are many places to choose from, from little trattorias to classy dining rooms. While Ristorante Metastasio tempts you with modern takes on classic Umbrian dishes, Il Frantoio, nestled in a historic olive mill, provides an outstanding menu made with regional ingredients.

Celebrating Christmas in Assisi - A Winter Wonderland

Assisi becomes a fairytale of lights, music, and tradition as winter descends over the city. Assisi's Christmas is a magical occasion. The town's profound religious traditions are visible in the exquisite nativity scenes and glittering lights that line the old streets. A magnificent Christmas tree and a midnight Mass that is filled with heavenly music make the Basilica of Saint Francis the focal point of the celebrations.

Locals and tourists assemble on Christmas Eve in the Piazza del Comune for a customary midnight feast. Seasonal treats include "capitone," a unique fried eel dish served on Christmas Eve, and "panettone," a sweet bread stuffed with candied fruit and raisins.

The charm of Assisi's Christmas spirit fills the streets as the clock strikes midnight. It's a time when the community's warmth, faith, and history come together to forge memories that will last well past the Christmas season. Your tour promises to be a rich tapestry of discovery and amazement with these encounters and a glimpse into Assisi's Christmas magic.

Enjoy every second of your journey!

Chapter 5

Itinerary Options

1 Day in Assisi: A Magical Day of Discovery

Morning: Explore History

San Francesco's Basilica (Upper and Lower Basilicas):

GPS Coordinates: 43.0704° N, 12.6190° E

Enter the Basilica of San Francesco to see the vibrant frescoes by world-famous painters Giotto and Cimabue. These works of art, which reflect the life of St. Francis, are more than just pictures; they are doors into another time.

Afternoon: Gastronomic Delights and Timeless Beauty

Enjoy Lunch at a neighbourhood Trattoria

GPS Coordinates (for a general area): 43.0704° N, 12.6190° E (Assisi's historic centre)

The local flavours are celebrated in Umbrian cuisine. Enjoy meals like wild boar stew and spaghetti with truffles before finishing with a decadent dessert.

1. Basilica di Santa Chiara:

GPS Coordinates: 43.0709° N, 12.6179° E

Take in the peace of the Santa Chiara Basilica. Its serene interior and softly coloured exterior evoke a sense of tranquillity and devotion.

2. Piazza del Comune (Minerva Temple)

GPS Coordinates: 43.0708° N, 12.6184° E

The Temple of Minerva is a Roman structure that can be found as you walk through Piazza del Comune. It has weathered the test of time. Its position in the middle of a mediaeval setting is evidence of Assisi's complex past.

Evening Suggestions: A Memorable Evening

Visit a local restaurant for dinner

GPS Coordinates (for a general area): 43.0704° N, 12.6190° E (Assisi's historic centre)

Enjoy a quiet meal in one of Assisi's charming eateries, where local wines and homely fare are expertly matched.

Take a leisurely evening stroll to Rocca Maggiore for a nighttime view

GPS Coordinates: 43.0681° N, 12.6146° E

Take a leisurely nighttime stroll around Assisi's cobblestone streets to cap off the day. Get yourself over to Rocca Maggiore for a beautiful perspective of Assisi lit up by stars and historic streetlamps at night.

2 Days in Assisi: Appreciate the History and the Beauty of Nature

Day 1: Exploring Historic Assisi

Morning: Follow the morning itinerary from Day 1 while exploring the Basilica of San Francesco's beauties.

Afternoon: Rocca Magna (GPS Coordinates: 43.0692° N, 12.6174° E)

While exploring Rocca Maggiore's historic walls, you can go on a time travel adventure in addition to taking in the panoramic views. Think of the kings and knights that once walked these ramparts.

Dinner at a Traditional Umbrian Restaurant

GPS Coordinates (for a general area): 43.0704° N, 12.6190° E (Assisi's historic centre)

Enjoy the delicious flavours of Umbria, where ancient dishes are lovingly and carefully prepared.

Day 2: The Natural Beauty and Spiritual Peace of Assisi

Morning: Eremo delle Carceri (GPS Coordinates: 43.0718° N, 12.6267° E)

Eremo delle Carceri offers a spiritual retreat in the serene woodlands outside of Assisi. Explore the tranquil hiking trails, take in the clean air, and be inspired where St. Francis found rest.

Enjoy Lunch at a Local Dining Spot

GPS Coordinates (for a general area): 43.0718° N, 12.6267° E (near Eremo delle Carceri)

Enjoy a delicious meal amidst the area's natural splendour, possibly on a terrace with views of the nearby hills.

Afternoon: Basilica di San Damiano (GPS Coordinates: 43.0730° N, 12.6071° E)

Visit the Basilica di San Damiano to see where St. Francis was called by God to "rebuild my church." This location's unassuming beauty exudes a sense of spiritual significance.

Free time: Take advantage of the late-afternoon wandering, local souvenir shopping, or simply lounging around Assisi.

Dinner: Finish your journey with a farewell meal while you think about Assisi's enchantment.

3 Days in Assisi: A Journey Through Time and Beauty

Assisi provides a diverse tapestry of natural beauty, history, and culture. You can explore this amazing town even more deeply if you have three days to spare. Here is a thorough schedule to help you make the most of your time:

Day 1: Historical Attractions

Morning: Visit the Basilica of San Francesco to start your day off well. While there, take time to see both the

Upper and Lower Basilicas as well as the magnificent murals by Giotto and Cimabue that decorate its walls.

GPS Coordinates: 43.0704° N, 12.6190° E

Lunch: In the heart of Assisi, have a leisurely lunch in an authentic trattoria or café.

GPS Coordinates (for a general area): 43.0704° N, 12.6190° E

Explore Rocca Maggiore, a mediaeval fortification that offers sweeping views of Assisi and the surrounding area, in the afternoon. Explore Assisi's past as you stroll around its historic walls. (*GPS Coordinates: 43.0692° N, 12.6174° E*)

Dinner: Indulge in a traditional Umbrian meal at a beautiful restaurant, tasting the mouthwatering flavours of the area.

GPS Coordinates (for a general area): 43.0704° N, 12.6190° E

Day 2: Soaking in the Countryside

Morning: Visit the Eremo delle Carceri, St. Francis's serene hermitage in the woods, to immerse yourself in Assisi's natural splendour. Discover serene hiking routes and spend time outdoors.

GPS Coordinates: 43.0718° N, 12.6267° E

Lunch: Savour exquisite Umbrian cuisine at a place tucked away in the lovely countryside.

Afternoon: Take in the splendour of the Bosco di San Francesco, a forest preserve that held a special place in St. Francis' heart. Hiking through the peaceful forests may lead you to secret springs and wildlife.

GPS Coordinates: 43.0674° N, 12.6092° E

Dinner: Choose from several restaurants serving both regional and global cuisine when you return to Assisi for dinner.

GPS Coordinates (for a general area): 43.0704° N, 12.6190° E

Day 3: Culture and the Arts

Morning: Visit the Basilica di Santa Chiara, which houses St. Clare's relics and features striking Gothic architecture, to start your cultural journey.

GPS Coordinates: 43.0709° N, 12.6179° E

Lunch: Indulge in a small meal while drinking espresso in a café that offers views of the charming town.

GPS Coordinates (for a general area): 43.0704° N, 12.6190° E

Afternoon: Explore the Roman Forum and Domus, two relics of Assisi's Roman past, before visiting the Basilica di San Pietro, a lesser-known wonder with exquisite frescoes.

- *GPS Coordinates (Basilica di San Pietro): 43.0667° N, 12.6114° E*
- *GPS Coordinates (Roman Forum and Domus): 43.0700° N, 12.6176° E*

Dinner: End your trip with a special farewell meal at a charming restaurant while enjoying Assisi's delectable cuisine.

GPS Coordinates (for a general area): 43.0704° N, 12.6190° E

Personalizing Your Journey

Family-Friendly Activities

- Consider paying a visit to the Porziuncola, a tiny chapel with significant historical and religious value, which is located inside the Basilica di Santa Maria degli Angeli. (*GPS Coordinates: 43.0622° N, 12.5675° E*)

- Visit the Bosco di San Francesco and have a picnic there for family-friendly entertainment. Kids can have fun on the outdoor playground.

Romantic Getaways

- Plan a relaxing horseback ride through the Umbrian countryside or a romantic picnic in the Bosco di San Francesco.

- Take a tour of a nearby vineyard and indulge in some of Umbria's best wines.

Itinerary for Adventure Seekers

- Set out on a bicycle expedition through the lovely villages and rolling hills that surround Assisi.
- Consider paragliding for an exhilarating experience and breathtaking vistas in the nearby Monte Subasio Regional Park.

Whether you're looking for exciting experiences, romantic getaways, or family-friendly activities, you can customise your trip to Assisi to suit your needs.

Everyone can find something exceptional in Assisi!

Chapter 6

Accomodation Options

Resorts and Hotels

★ *Giotto Hotel & Spa (GPS Coordinates: 43.0712° N, 12.6094° E):* An opulent choice with lovely rooms, a spa, and a rooftop terrace providing panoramic views. Cost range: €150–€250 per night.

★ *Hotel Cenacolo:* Near the Basilica of San Francesco is the beautiful guesthouse Cenacolo. Cost range: €100–200 per night. *You can book online at:* https://www.hotelcenacolo.com/ *(Address: Viale Patrono d'Italia, 70, 06081 Assisi (Italia))*

★ *Grand Hotel Assisi (GPS Coordinates: 43.0602° N, 12.6297° E):* The Grand Hotel Assisi is a four-star establishment featuring tasteful accommodations, a pool, and a restaurant serving Umbrian food. Cost range: €120–220 per night.

Inns And Guesthouses

- *Le Case (GPS Coordinates: 43.0714° N, 12.6179° E)*: A charming inn with comfortable accommodations and friendly staff. Cost range: €60–€100 per night.

- *B&B Assisana (GPS Coordinates: 43.0613° N, 12.5891° E)*: A delightful bed and breakfast with cosy accommodations and a welcoming atmosphere is B&B Assisana. Cost range: €50–€90 per night.

- *Casa Leonori (GPS Coordinates: 43.0613° N, 12.5891° E)*: Casa Leonori is a family-run bed and breakfast renowned for its friendliness and delectable homemade breakfast. Cost range: €70–120 per night.

Hostels And Cheap Lodgings

→ (Ostello Victor Centre GPS Coordinates: 43.0693°
N, 12.6176° E): Ostello Victor Centre is a hostel
that is affordable and has tidy rooms and a common
kitchen. Cost range: €20–€50 per night.

→ Assisi Hostel: Another affordable choice with
dormitory-style rooms and a friendly ambience is
the Assisi Hostel—cost range: €20 to €45 per
night.

Assisi Transportation

Getting To Assisi

★ *Perugia San Francesco d'Assisi Airport (PEG):* Taxi
costs to Assisi from Perugia San Francesco d'Assisi
Airport (PEG) range from €20 to €30, while bus

tickets cost between €8 and €10 each. The trip takes 20 to 30 minutes.

★ *From Rome:* From Roma Termini station, you can take a train to Assisi if you are flying into Rome's Fiumicino Airport (FCO). The trip takes about 2.5 to 3 hours, and the ticket costs about €20 to €30.

Navigating Assisi

Assisi is a pedestrian town, and most of its attractions are nearby. For short excursions within Assisi, taxis run between €10 and €20. The cost of a public bus within the town is between €1 and €2.

Retail and Souvenir Shops

Local Markets

Fresh food, cheese, and local delicacies are available in the Mercato Coperto for affordable prices. Budget between €20 and €30 for a moderate shopping trip.

Gift Stores

Small trinkets and premium pottery are both available at Assisi's souvenir shops. The cost of a common memento might range from $5 to $20.

Language Hints And Practical Phrases

Although Italian is the primary language of Assisi, you can hear English being used in tourist areas. For a more immersive experience, learning a few fundamental phrases is beneficial.

Medical Services and Emergency Contacts

For general emergencies, such as police, fire, and medical aid, call 112 instead of calling 911.

The Santa Maria degli Angeli Hospital is the closest hospital and a medical consultation without insurance may cost between €50 and €100. Make sure you have travel insurance to pay for any unanticipated medical costs you may incur while travelling.

You should be able to plan your vacation to Assisi while staying within your budget with these projected prices and logistical information. Enjoy your time in this lovely town!

Language Hints And Practical Phrases

While English is widely spoken among Assisians who work in the tourism sector, learning a few simple

Italian words can improve your trip and demonstrate respect for the local way of life. The following are some language and phrase suggestions:

Basic Expressions

- Hello: Ciao (chow)
- Good morning: Buongiorno (bwohn-JOHR-noh)
- Good afternoon/evening: Buonasera (bwoh-nah-SEH-rah)
- Good night: Buonanotte (bwoh-nah-NOH-teh)
- Thank you: Grazie (GRAH-tsyeh)
- Please: Per favore (pehr fah-VOH-reh)
- Yes: Sì (SEE)
- No: No (noh)
- Excuse me / Sorry: Mi scusi (mee SKOO-zee)
- Do you speak English?: Parla inglese? (PAR-lah een-GLEH-zeh)

Language Tips

- Politeness: Italians value manners. Always introduce yourself and use the words "please" (per favore) and "thank you" (grazie) when necessary.

- Learn Basic Numbers: Learn Numbers 1 through 10 so you can comprehend costs and quantities whether you are dining or shopping.

- Useful Expressions: Although English is widely spoken by Italians in tourist areas, it can still be useful to know a few basic expressions, especially if you travel off the main path.

- Pronunciation: Pay attention to how words are said because Italian pronunciation can vary from English pronunciation. If you can, practise with residents of the area.

- Language Apps: Consider using phrasebooks or language learning apps to brush up on your Italian and improve your vacation experience.

By embracing the local tongue and culture, you can deepen your vacation experience by connecting with Assisi's residents and learning a few basic Italian phrases. Enjoy learning new languages in this charming city!

Chapter 7

Insider Tips For First-Timers

Moving Through Lines and Crowds

- *Visit Early or Late:* Arrange your trips during early morning or later evening hours to avoid crowds at major locations like the Basilica of San Francesco. Most tourists arrive in the midday hours.

- *Book Tickets in Advance:* Consider purchasing tickets online in advance for big attractions when booking tickets. You can avoid standing in line for tickets by doing this.

- *Discover Lesser-Known Gems:* Assisi offers more than just its well-known sights. Discover the town's quieter and more private side by exploring smaller churches, lanes, and vistas.

Saving Money on Your Trip

- *Eat Where the Locals Do:* Look for trattorias and osterias that are popular with the community. Authentic Italian food can frequently be found for less money than in eateries that cater to tourists.

- *Shop at Local Markets:* Visit neighbourhood markets like the Mercato Coperto for fresh food, cheese, and other treats. It is not merely an affordable cultural experience.

- *Use Public Transportation:* If you need to get around Assisi, think about using the neighbourhood bus or going on foot. It saves money and enables unhurried exploration of the town. You will also get to interact with locals and see other beautiful structures along the way.

Getting to Know the Community

- *Learn some basic Italian words:* Communicating with natives can be greatly improved by learning even a few simple Italian words. This kind of effort is valued by the locals, and it may result in more enjoyable talks.

- *Be Respectful in Churches:* Remember that churches are places of worship when you visit them and treat them with respect. To demonstrate respect for the sacred environment, dress modestly, keep your voice down, and switch off your phone.

- *Ask for advice:* Don't be afraid to seek out advice from locals about eateries, secret spots, or unusual activities. They can offer insightful information that manuals might overlook.

Maximising Your Visit

- *Get Immersed in History:* Assisi is a city rich in history. Explore its historic sites at your own pace, and think about hiring a local guide to learn more about the town's fascinating past.

- *Discover Umbrian Cuisine:* Umbria is renowned for its delicious cuisine. For a genuine experience of the area, try local specialities including truffle meals, Umbrian olive oil, and local wines.

- *Attend festivals and events:* Determine whether any festivals or events are scheduled to take place while you are there. Every year, Assisi plays host to many religious and cultural festivals that provide visitors with a fascinating look at the city's customs.

You'll not only get the most out of your vacation to Assisi by using these insider suggestions, but you'll also fully experience the town's culture, history, and charm while saving money and avoiding the crowds. Enjoy this exquisite Italian jewel and your amazing experience!

Assisi Village, Italy

Conclusion

Assisi lures visitors to explore its winding lanes, see historic churches and savour the flavours of Umbrian cuisine because of its timeless beauty, extensive history, and spiritual significance. This charming town offers an out-of-the-ordinary experience since it is tucked away among undulating hills and olive trees. Consider the following as you make travel plans to Assisi:

★ Discover the historical gems, including the Basilica of San Francesco and the quaint lanes that are filled with historical tales.

★ Engage in conversation with locals, even if it's simply a friendly "Buongiorno." A memorable discovery may result from their advice and ideas.

★ For a true taste of the region's gastronomic heritage, savour the local food, from truffle-infused meals to the best Umbrian wines.

★ Utilise smart crowd management techniques by going to major locations during off-peak times and appreciating the lesser-known jewels that make Assisi unique.

★ Take part in local celebrations and festivals while immersing yourself in Assisi's spirituality and culture.

Remember that Assisi will leave an indelible stamp on your heart as you set off on your adventure. It's a location where spirituality and history converge, where the beauty of nature coexists with historical artistic creations, and where the friendliness of its inhabitants makes you feel at home right away.

Assisi has countless beauties just waiting to be discovered, making every trip a singular and enlightening experience, whether you're a first-time tourist or returning to this lovely town.

Happy travels! (Safe journeys!)

Bonus Information: 30 Exciting Things To Do in Assisi

★ **Tour the Basilica of San Francesco:** Visit the Upper and Lower Basilicas of the Basilica of San Francesco to see the beautiful frescoes by Giotto and Cimabue.

★ **Hike to Eremo delle Carceri:** Hike to St. Francis's serene hermitage in the forests outside of Assisi at Eremo delle Carceri.

★ **Visit the Basilica di Santa Chiara:** Explore the Basilica di Santa Chiara to take in its peaceful exterior and rose-coloured interior.

★ **Wander through Piazza del Comune:** Explore Assisi's historic centre by strolling through Piazza del Comune and viewing the Minerva Temple from Roman times.

★ **Climb Rocca Maggiore:** Ascend Rocca Maggiore for sweeping views of Assisi and the surrounding area.

★ **Discover the Roman Forum and Domus:** Visit the Roman Forum and Domus to learn more about Assisi's Roman past.

★ **Explore the Bosco di San Francesco:** Hike through the tranquil woods where St Francis sought comfort as you explore the Bosco di San Francesco.

★ **Picnic at the Hermitage:** Have a picnic at the Eremo delle Carceri or in the lovely countryside.

★ **Attend a Local Festival:** Calendimaggio, which features mediaeval reenactments, is a festival where you may learn about the culture of Assisi.

★ **Eat Umbrian cuisine:** At a neighbourhood trattoria, savour delicacies topped with Umbrian olive oil, wild boar stew, and truffle-infused pasta.

★ **Take a Cooking Class:** Attend a cooking class to learn how to make typical Umbrian meals and uncover the secrets of true Italian food.

★ **Wine Tasting in a Vineyard:** Enjoy Umbrian wines and local cheeses at a nearby vineyard.

★ **Shop for Ceramics:** Look for beautiful ceramics and hand-painted pottery in artisan stores.

★ **Attend a Gregorian Chant Performance:** Attend a Gregorian Chant Performance to hear the ethereal sound of these chants used in religious events.

★ **Explore the Streets at Night:** Take a leisurely nighttime stroll through Assisi's lit cobblestone streets.

★ **Visit the Porziuncola:** Look at the Basilica of Santa Maria degli Angeli, which contains the Porziuncola chapel.

★ **Participate in Artisan Workshops:** Attend workshops where regional craftsmen showcase their talents, from making ceramics to producing olive oil.

★ **Admire Local Art Galleries:** Explore Modern and Classical Art in Assisi's Galleries, Showcasing Local and International Artists.

★ **Capture Sunsets:** From sweeping vantage points, observe the sun setting over Assisi's beautiful surroundings.

★ **Take a Hot Air Balloon Ride:** Experience breathtaking views as you soar over the Umbrian countryside in a hot air balloon.

★ **Visit the Hermitage of the Carceri Monastery:** Explore the Hermitage of the Carceri Monastery to explore the tranquil, lushly forested monastic complex.

★ **Attend Mass at the Basilica of San Francesco:** Get immersed at the Mass in the Basilica of San Francesco to connect spiritually.

★ **Explore the Basilica di San Damiano:** Discover the modest beauty of the Basilica of San Damiano, where St. Francis received a divine call.

★ **Stroll Along the Via San Francesco:** Stroll through Via San Francesco to browse gift shops and take in live street entertainment.

★ **Take a Day Trip to Perugia:** Visit the neighbouring city of Perugia for a day trip; it is well-known for its mediaeval centre and chocolate making.

★ **Admire the St. Clare Porch:** Take in the delicate elements of the porch at the Basilica di Santa Chiara.

★ **Explore the Civic Museum:** Visit the Civic Museum to learn about Assisi's history and art.

★ **Discover the Rocca Minore:** Explore the Rocca Minore for even more breathtaking views of Assisi.

★ **Attend a Live Music Performance:** Look into any concerts or other musical activities taking place in the area while you're there.

★ **Take a Guided Tour:** A skilled local guide can help you better grasp Assisi's history and culture.

Assisi delivers a rich and rewarding experience with these 30 intriguing activities, fusing history, culture, nature, and gastronomy for a unique adventure. Enjoy your exploration of this alluring Italian city!

Printed in Great Britain
by Amazon

41814621R00050